DESTINATION SPACE

SPACE STATIONS

by Christa C. Hogan

FOCUS READERS

www.focusreaders.com

Focus Readers is distributed by North Star Editions:
sales@northstareditions.com | 888-417-0195

Produced for Focus Readers by Red Line Editorial.

Content Consultant: Dr. David A. Weintraub, Professor of Astronomy, Department of Physics & Astronomy, Vanderbilt University

Photographs ©: JSC/NASA, cover, 1, 9, 10–11, 14–15, 17, 19, 20–21, 27, 28–29, 31, 33, 34–35, 37, 39, 41, 42–43; MSFC/NASA, 4–5, 13, 22; Sovfoto/AP Images, 7; NASA, 25; Red Line Editorial, 45

ISBN
978-1-63517-499-1 (hardcover)
978-1-63517-571-4 (paperback)
978-1-63517-715-2 (ebook pdf)
978-1-63517-643-8 (hosted ebook)

Library of Congress Control Number: 2017948054

Printed in the United States of America
Mankato, MN
November, 2017

ABOUT THE AUTHOR

Christa C. Hogan writes nonfiction for children and adults. She lives in North Carolina with her husband and their three boys.

TABLE OF CONTENTS

CHAPTER 1

INTO ORBIT

The alarm clock beeps, and the astronaut floats out of her sleeping pod. She squirts water droplets from a tube and brushes her teeth. Then she spits the toothpaste into a towel. After breakfast, she will conduct an experiment in the space station's research lab. But first, she stops to look out a window. Earth floats like a pale blue ball far below. After two years of training for her mission, she is excited to finally be in space.

Astronaut Ellen Ochoa looks out a window of the International Space Station in 2002.

Space stations are large structures in space where astronauts live and work. Since the 1970s, humans have built several space stations that **orbit** Earth. Many countries have sent astronauts to live in these stations for days, weeks, or even months. These longer stays allow scientists to study how living in space affects the human body.

The Soviet Union built the first space station in 1971. Known as Salyut 1, it launched into space on April 19. Two days later, a Soyuz space shuttle carried three **cosmonauts** into space. The shuttle docked, or connected, with Salyut 1. However, the cosmonauts could not open the station's hatch, so they had to return to Earth.

Another Soyuz shuttle carried a new crew to Salyut 1 in June 1971. This time, the cosmonauts were able to open the hatch and enter the station. They spent three weeks in space. While they were

▲ An artist's illustration of a Soyuz shuttle (left) preparing to dock with Salyut 1 (right)

on the space station, the cosmonauts orbited Earth 383 times. However, tragedy struck during their return flight. An air leak **depressurized** the shuttle, and all three cosmonauts died.

Salyut 1 orbited Earth for a total of 175 days. Then Soviet scientists fired the empty space station's engines, pushing it into a lower orbit. From there, Salyut 1 fell toward Earth and splashed into the Pacific Ocean.

Despite the deaths of the three cosmonauts, the Soviet Union sent six more Salyut stations into space. Each new space station used an improved design. But all of the stations stayed in a fairly low orbit around Earth. This low orbit made each station easy to reach with space shuttles. However, it also meant the station was still inside Earth's upper atmosphere. As the space station moved through the atmosphere, **drag** lowered the station's orbit. The station needed booster rockets to move it back up to a slightly higher orbit. Otherwise, the station would fall back to Earth.

▲ Soyuz shuttles continued to carry passengers and cargo to several other space stations.

Salyut 7 was the last space station of its kind. The last crew visited Salyut 7 in 1986. The Soviet Union's government struggled in the late 1980s. It could not afford any more repairs or shuttles. Left unused for several years, Salyut 7 fell to Earth in 1991. Most of the station burned up as it reentered Earth's atmosphere. However, the technology used to build it paved the way for future space stations.

CHAPTER 2

SKYLAB

eanwhile, scientists in the United States were hard at work. The National Aeronautics and Space Administration (NASA) launched a space station known as Skylab in 1973. Skylab held laboratories, workshops, and a living space. It also carried a large solar telescope. From 1973 to 1974, three crews visited Skylab. The astronauts spent a total of 171 days aboard the station. They used it to study Earth and the sun.

Skylab was more than three and a half times the size of Salyut 1.

The astronauts also did experiments, such as mixing metals and growing crystals. This helped them see how materials would behave in space.

In addition, astronauts studied how longer stays in space affected the human body. In particular, they studied the effects of **microgravity**. Microgravity on a space station causes the people and objects inside it to seem weightless. On Earth, a person's muscles and bones must resist gravity. That is not the case in microgravity. Scientists needed to study how astronauts' bodies would react. They learned that microgravity can weaken muscles and bones.

> **THINK ABOUT IT**

How else might microgravity affect astronauts on a space station?

▲ Astronaut Owen Garriott works on Skylab's solar telescope in 1973.

Originally, Skylab was built to last for eight to ten years after the last astronauts visited it. NASA planned to use a shuttle to push the empty space station into a higher orbit. Then Skylab could orbit Earth permanently with other space **debris**. But NASA did not have the money to send a shuttle. Instead, NASA fired Skylab's rockets to push it toward Earth in 1979. Skylab broke apart as it entered the atmosphere. Still, it had helped NASA learn how humans could live safely in orbit.

CHAPTER 3

THE MIR SPACE STATION

Next, the Soviet Union designed a large space station. Known as Mir, this space station could hold enough supplies for cosmonauts to live in space for more than a year. In fact, Mir was so large that it had to be launched in pieces. The first piece, or module, was launched in 1986. Five more modules were added during the next decade. Spacecraft brought the modules to space, where astronauts connected them together.

When it was completed in 1996, Mir was 62 feet (19 m) long and 102 feet (31 m) wide.

Building and using space stations is risky. A space station must contain everything the astronauts need during their stay. If the station loses supplies such as air, water, or food, it can no longer support life.

For example, Mir's crew faced a major problem in February 1997. A faulty oxygen canister started a fire. Mir's fans, which moved air throughout the station to keep it fresh, helped the fire spread quickly. Mir's crew put out the fire, but the station filled with toxic smoke. The crew wore gas masks while the station's life-support system cleared the smoke. Fortunately, no one was hurt.

In June 1997, Mir crew members tried to dock a Progress supply shuttle with the station. But they could view the shuttle only by video. This made it difficult to judge how fast the shuttle was moving. Instead of docking, the shuttle crashed into Mir's

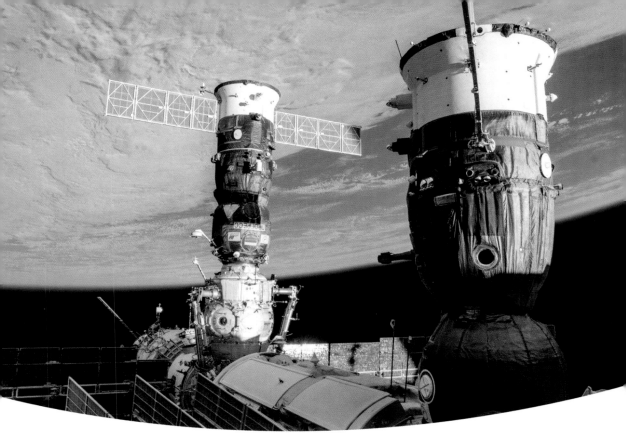

⚠ A Progress supply shuttle (left) is approximately the size of a school bus.

solar panels and punctured a science lab module. The crash threw Mir into an uncontrolled spin.

The space station lost half its power and leaked air. Crew members rushed to repair it. They sealed off the leaking module to preserve their oxygen. And they fired Mir's engines to stop the spinning.

Fortunately, no one was injured. But Mir lost many of its scientific experiments.

Scientists hoped to learn how humans could live for a long time in space. They needed to study the effects of microgravity, which they could only observe while people were in orbit. Valeri Polyakov set the record for the longest time spent in space when he stayed aboard Mir for 437 days. Scientists studied how this affected his health.

Mir scientists also learned that microgravity affected plants and animals. The scientists grew wheat plants. The seeds grew in containers that carefully controlled the amount of light, humidity, and nutrition the plants received. Scientists hoped seeds from these plants could be used to grow more wheat. But even though the wheat plants matured, they did not produce seeds. Mir scientists studied the development of quail as

⬙ Growing plants in space is called astroculture.

well. The birds hatched from eggs on the station. But as they grew, they suffered serious defects.

Mir orbited Earth for 15 years. During that time, the Soviet Union dissolved. It was easier for NASA to work with the new government of Russia. Russia later joined a team of nations that worked together to create a new kind of space station.

CHAPTER 4

BUILDING THE INTERNATIONAL SPACE STATION

The United States had begun plans for a space station in the 1980s. But in 1993, the country agreed to work with Russia on a new plan. Space agencies from Canada, Europe, and Japan also helped build this new space station. Called the International Space Station (ISS), it was made up of more than 100 pieces that were launched separately. The first piece was launched in 1998. More than 40 missions carried pieces into space.

The space shuttle *Endeavour* carried the second piece of the ISS to space on December 4, 1998.

▲ In 2000, the ISS had only three modules.

Astronauts connected the pieces together while in orbit. By the time the ISS was finished in 2011, 15 countries had helped build it.

The ISS is much larger than previous space stations. Other stations could hold only two or three astronauts at a time. But the ISS can hold as many as ten. In fact, it was the largest structure ever built in space. The ISS has the wingspan of a football field. On Earth, it would weigh nearly 1 million pounds (453,600 kg).

The ISS is made up of a series of modules shaped like canisters and spheres. Astronauts live and work inside these modules. The modules are attached to a main truss, which is a long metal beam. The truss acts as the backbone of the space station. Giant solar panels and heat radiators extend from the truss like wings. The solar panels convert sunlight into electricity. Heat radiators release extra heat from the sun's rays and the ISS's electronic systems.

A large robotic arm helps space shuttles dock with the ISS. This arm also moves supplies delivered by shuttles from Earth. It can even help build parts of the station or move astronauts as they are working outside.

The ISS travels around Earth at a speed of 17,500 miles per hour (28,200 km/h). It orbits 248 miles (400 km) above the ground. Many pieces of space debris also orbit Earth at this height. NASA tracks more than 500,000 pieces of space debris. Some pieces are larger than softballs. Others are as small as marbles. These objects travel at 17,500 miles per hour (28,200 km/h). At that speed, even a tiny speck of debris could damage the ISS.

Debris shields protect the ISS from small collisions. When larger debris approaches the ISS, the station's crew has several options. If time allows, crew members can use booster rockets to move the ISS out of the way. But sometimes they do not have enough time to move the space station. In these cases, crew members can retreat to the Soyuz shuttle. This shuttle is always attached to the ISS. The crew could use it to return to Earth if the ISS were seriously damaged. But in most cases, a combination of careful planning, tracking space debris, and using debris shields can prevent a major collision.

ISS PARTS ◁

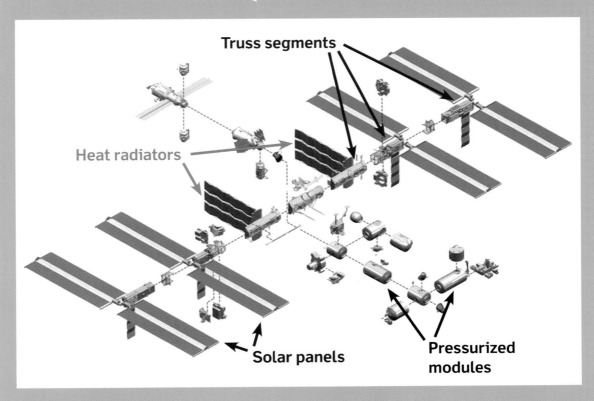

Truss segments

Heat radiators

Solar panels

Pressurized modules

SPACE ROBOTS

Several robots help astronauts with their work on the ISS. For example, a robotic arm slides along the station's truss. An astronaut uses two controllers to operate the arm from inside the station. Cameras and computer monitors allow the astronaut to see the arm as it moves. Each end of the arm can attach to fixtures on the outside of the ISS. When one end of the arm is attached, the other end can move freely. This end can also bend and attach to a different part of the station. Then the first end lets go. This allows the arm to move around the ISS, similar to the way an inchworm moves.

Robonaut 2 is another robot aboard the ISS. This robot has fingers and hands that work much like a human's. For this reason, the robot can use astronauts' tools to perform basic maintenance. This frees the astronauts to focus on more

▲ Robonaut 2 is operated by remote control.

critical tasks. Scientists planned for Robonaut 2 to someday be able to perform space walks and repairs that are risky for humans.

Smaller robots, known as Astrobees, were also designed for the ISS. Each of these cube-shaped robots is the size of a toaster oven. They contain cameras, sensors, and computers. Astrobees are designed to propel themselves around the ISS, taking videos and running tests set up by humans.

CHAPTER 5

LIFE IN SPACE

Astronauts have lived and worked on the ISS continually since November 2000. But life in space is not easy for the human body. The ISS must protect astronauts from harmful radiation, such as extreme ultraviolet light, X-rays, and giant solar flares. Humans on Earth are exposed to small amounts of harmful radiation from the sun's rays. However, Earth's atmosphere protects humans from most of the dangerous radiation.

Roberto Vittori floats through the ISS's *Destiny* laboratory.

Astronauts in space are not protected by Earth's atmosphere. As a result, they are exposed to much more radiation. This added exposure can cause many serious health problems. Space stations such as the ISS use radiation shields to protect the astronauts. Physicians on Earth carefully monitor astronauts' radiation levels as well.

Microgravity is also hard on the human body. After many days in a weightless environment, humans lose bone and muscle strength. To prevent this, ISS astronauts spend more than two hours exercising every day. They use tension equipment that is designed to resist their movements and help them stay strong.

> ## ➤ THINK ABOUT IT

What else must the ISS protect astronauts from?

Astronaut Koichi Wakata exercises using the Advanced Resistive Exercise Device.

Astronauts may also take medicine to help keep their bones healthy.

In addition, the stress of entering a new environment makes astronauts more likely to get sick. So, the ISS is designed to keep astronauts healthy and comfortable. The station's lighting is similar to light on Earth. This helps the astronauts' bodies know when it is time to rest.

Plus, the station's internal temperature is kept constant so the astronauts will not get too hot or too cold.

Many people live close together on the ISS. They can easily share germs. To prevent this, air on the ISS is filtered to keep it clean. Also, all supplies sent to the ISS are sterilized before they leave Earth. This process prevents new germs and bacteria from entering the space station. However, germs and bacteria do still exist on the station.

Astronauts also need water. But water is heavy. Instead of always shipping water from Earth, 93 percent of the water the ISS uses is recycled. A water recovery system pulls moisture from the ISS environment. Sweat, **condensation**, and urine are recycled into clean drinking water.

On Earth, toilets use water to flush away waste. Toilets on the ISS use air instead. The air

▲ Because of microgravity, water droplets can float throughout the ISS.

sucks urine and solid waste away. The urine is recycled. Solid waste is bundled and shot into space. Gravity pulls the bundles back toward Earth, where they burn up in the atmosphere. If no bathroom is available, such as during space walks or the trip to and from Earth, astronauts wear adult diapers.

CHAPTER 6

ABOARD THE ISS

More than 200 different astronauts from more than 15 countries have visited the ISS. Together, they have performed hundreds of experiments. Many of these experiments will pave the way for deep space exploration to places such as Mars. In 2015, for example, ISS astronauts grew, harvested, and ate lettuce for the first time. They are now closer to creating sustainable food sources for longer missions.

Peggy Whitson holds an experiment growing soybeans aboard the ISS in 2002.

ISS research also benefits people on Earth. For instance, the space station's robotic arm inspired engineers to develop a robotic arm that assists surgeons during difficult procedures. And ISS medical research is contributing to the treatment of muscular dystrophy and bone loss. In addition, the ISS takes many images of Earth. Studying these images helps scientists measure the effects of natural disasters such as floods and volcanic eruptions.

Floating around all day on the ISS may look easy, but microgravity makes many activities difficult. For example, food can float off an

> **THINK ABOUT IT**

In what ways would growing food aboard a space station be different than growing food on Earth?

⬈ Tacos, hamburgers, and even lasagna are often on the menu at the ISS.

astronaut's plate. In the 1960s, astronauts ate **pureed** food from tubes. Scientists also tried freeze-drying food, but astronauts complained about the taste and texture. Today, astronauts eat some of the same meals as people on Earth.

But astronauts' food must be carefully chosen and prepared. Some foods, such as meats, can contain harmful bacteria. Scientists must test and approve each meal to make sure the astronauts do not get sick.

Floating food could damage parts of the ISS. For this reason, astronauts often eat moist foods. The increased **surface tension** in space helps these foods stick to a plate and fork. Salt and pepper are made into liquids to prevent tiny pieces from floating away. Water droplets could also damage ISS equipment. So, astronauts drink water from sealed pouches. They must be careful to not let any water escape. They also use shampoos and soaps that need less water.

Although ISS astronauts work hard, they do have free time. On weekends, they read, watch movies, and play games. Astronauts can also use

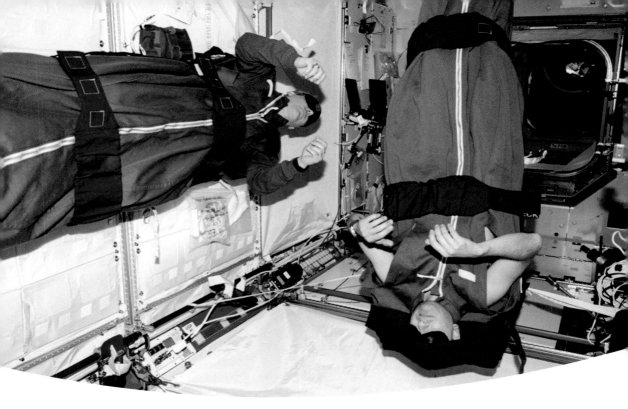

⚠ Astronauts Thomas Jones and Mark Polansky are strapped in their sleep stations in the *Destiny* laboratory.

their computers to call their families. Watching Earth through a window is another favorite way to pass the time.

Each astronaut has a private sleep station. This sleep station holds the astronaut's personal items and sleeping bag. At night, astronauts zip into their sleeping bags so they will not float away.

LELAND MELVIN

Leland Melvin loved science when he was a boy. However, he did not dream of being an astronaut. Melvin was black. He saw only white astronauts in books and on television. So he did not think someone like himself could go to space.

When Melvin grew up, he became a player in the National Football League. However, an injury ended his career early. After retiring, he went back to college to study math, science, and engineering. While in school, Melvin met a NASA scientist who encouraged him to become an astronaut.

Melvin trained for many years to become an astronaut. While training, he suffered another injury. He lost most of the hearing in one ear. He was told he would not be able to go to space. Even so, Melvin continued training. He finally regained his hearing and was given permission to go to

▲ Packages of food float around Leland Melvin on the flight deck of the *Atlantis* space shuttle.

space. In 2008, Melvin flew in the space shuttle *Atlantis* and went to work on the ISS. He returned to the ISS in 2009.

After retiring from NASA in 2014, Melvin began traveling around the United States to encourage girls and people of color to study math and science. He wants kids to know that anyone can become an astronaut with hard work and dedication.

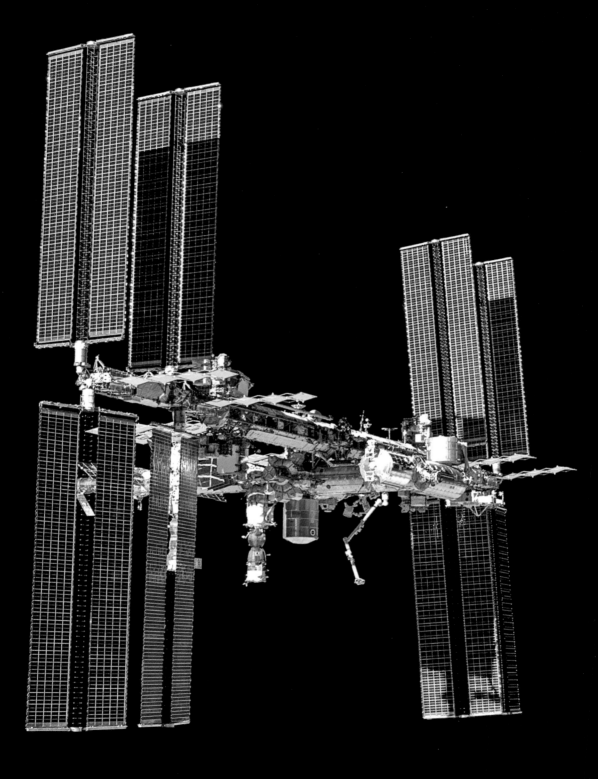

CHAPTER 7

LOOKING AHEAD

Keeping a space station in orbit is expensive. For example, NASA spent more than $3 billion on the ISS in 2016. Space agencies from Canada, Europe, Japan, Russia, and the United States have agreed to contribute to the ISS until 2024. After that, the space agencies could decide to retire the ISS. Or, private companies might take over running the ISS. The companies could send their own spacecraft or modules to the station.

The ISS orbits Earth every 90 minutes.

Russia has even discussed using its country's modules to build a new space station.

China worked to build its own space station as well. The country launched a **prototype**, known as Tiangong 1, in 2011. A second prototype, Tiangong 2, was sent to orbit in 2016. China planned to add more modules to Tiangong 2 to create a permanent space station in the 2020s.

NASA also made plans to build a new, smaller space station in the 2020s. This station is designed to orbit the moon. It could bring astronauts deeper into space than ever before. NASA might even use the space station to carry astronauts all the way to Mars.

Even if the ISS is retired, space stations will continue to be an important part of space exploration. As scientists share information and resources, new technology will enable humans to

stay in space for longer periods of time. One day,
they may even be able to live there permanently.

SPACE STATION STATS ◄

Station Name	Launch Date	Reentry Date	Total Visitors
Salyut 1	April 19, 1971	October 11, 1971	3
Salyut 2	April 3, 1973	May 28, 1973	0
Skylab	May 14, 1973	July 11, 1979	9
Salyut 3	June 24, 1974	January 24, 1975	2
Salyut 4	December 26, 1974	February 2, 1977	4
Salyut 5	June 22, 1976	August 28, 1977	4
Salyut 6	September 29, 1977	July 29, 1982	33
Salyut 7	April 19, 1982	February 7, 1991	22
Mir	February 19, 1986	March 23, 2001	125
ISS	November 20, 1998	—	228*

*Total visitors to the ISS as of September 2017

FOCUS ON
SPACE STATIONS

Write your answers on a separate piece of paper.

1. Write three paragraphs describing how astronauts deal with microgravity while they are living on the ISS.

2. Would you want to spend a year living on a space station? Why or why not?

3. Which country sent the first space station into orbit?
- A. the Soviet Union
- B. the United States
- C. China

4. Why would microgravity cause astronauts to lose muscle strength?
- A. Their muscles get too worn out from the hard work of moving around the space station.
- B. The food astronauts eat does not contain enough protein to keep their muscles strong.
- C. Their muscles no longer have to work as hard to resist gravity, so they become weaker.

Answer key on page 48.

GLOSSARY

condensation
Water that gathers into droplets on surfaces that are cooler than the air.

cosmonauts
Astronauts from the Soviet Union or Russia.

debris
The remains of something broken.

depressurized
Caused part of an airplane or spacecraft to no longer be sealed off, so that the air pressure in that part cannot be kept at safe levels for people inside it.

drag
The force of air pushing back against a moving object.

microgravity
When the downward pull of gravity is very small compared with the forward motion of an object such as a space station.

orbit
To repeatedly follow a curved path around another object because of gravity.

prototype
An early version of an invention that is created to test an idea.

pureed
Crushed until it becomes a thick liquid or paste.

surface tension
The thin, stretchy film at the edge of a liquid that keeps the molecules in the liquid together.

TO LEARN MORE

BOOKS

Grayson, Robert. *Exploring Space*. Minneapolis: Abdo Publishing, 2014.

Jones, Tom. *Ask the Astronaut: A Galaxy of Astonishing Answers to Your Questions on Spaceflight*. Washington, DC: Smithsonian Books, 2016.

Melvin, Leland. *Chasing Space: Young Readers' Edition*. New York: Amistad, 2017.

NOTE TO EDUCATORS

Visit **www.focusreaders.com** to find lesson plans, activities, links, and other resources related to this title.

INDEX

Answer Key: 1. Answers will vary; **2.** Answers will vary; **3.** A; **4.** C